April 1980

UR:
THE FIRST PHASES

UR:
THE FIRST PHASES

By

LEONARD WOOLLEY

The KING PENGUIN *Books*
PUBLISHED BY PENGUIN BOOKS LIMITED
LONDON *and* NEW YORK
1946

THE KING PENGUIN BOOKS

Editor : N. B. L. Pevsner
Technical Editor : R. B. Fishenden

First published 1946

MADE IN GREAT BRITAIN

Text Pages printed by
R. & R. CLARK, LTD., EDINBURGH
Set in Monotype Bembo

Colour Plates
Made and Printed by JOHN SWAIN & SON, LTD.

Cover design by
WILLIAM GRIMMOND

PUBLISHED BY

PENGUIN BOOKS LTD.
HARMONDSWORTH MIDDLESEX
ENGLAND

PENGUIN BOOKS INC.
245 FIFTH AVENUE
NEW YORK

To

MY WIFE

who helped me alike in the ex-
cavation of the Royal Tombs and
in the writing of this essay

ACKNOWLEDGMENTS

The plates are reproduced by the kind permission of the Trustees of the British Museum and of the Museum of the University of Pennsylvania

UR:

THE FIRST PHASES

NEARLY all the plates in this book illustrate treasures found in the Royal Tombs of Ur. But when faced with a strange and ancient civilisation which could produce works of art so rich and technically so perfect, we naturally ask how it arose; and so the text deals mainly with the history of Ur before the time of the Royal Tombs. That really means the early history of the land of Sumer, or southern Mesopotamia; and if in what follows little but Ur is mentioned, it must not be forgotten that our historical knowledge is derived from many sources and from the labours of many archaeologists on many sites. No one site has produced a consecutive record illustrated equally well in all its phases; there are always gaps which must be filled in from results obtained elsewhere. By piecing those results together we can set in order the stages by which Sumerian civilisation advanced from its crude beginning in the Late Stone Age to the fine flower of the dynasties which ruled over an urbanised and an urbane realm.

We are dealing with prehistoric times. Therefore we cannot ask for dated history; we must be content with successive periods whose individual character is clearly marked but whose length in time remains quite unknown. Here we are concerned with five such stages, each of which is named by archaeologists after the place where the first evidence of it was discovered.

The earliest is the al 'Ubaid Period. Al 'Ubaid was a small settlement, four miles north of Ur, where was first noted the painted pottery which characterises all the very early sites of Sumer.

Next comes the Uruk Period, first made known by the excavations at Warka, forty miles north of Ur, the site of the ancient city which in the Bible is called Erech and in Babylonian texts Uruk.

The third stage is the Jemdet Nasr Period, named after a little mound east of Hillah (which is Babylon) where a new type of pottery was found associated with clay tablets written in an archaic script.

To Jemdet Nasr succeeds the Early Dynastic Period. Now for the first time a skeleton of history is furnished by the 'King-Lists', drawn up by the Sumerian scribes about 2000 B.C.; they give the names of the rulers of the various dynasties which in turn claimed suzerainty over the land of Sumer. To this period belong the royal tombs of Ur and also the First Dynasty of Ur, whose historical existence was vouched for by the discovery, in the temple at al 'Ubaid, of a foundation-stone bearing the names of two of its kings.

The Early Dynastic Period ends with the rise to power of Sargon, the great king of Akkad, or northern Mesopotamia. He can be dated approximately to 2560 B.C. From his time onward we deal not with stages of history but with a chronology reckoned in years.

For the early history two factors are of prime importance: the land and the people. Man must adapt himself to his surroundings, even while he masters them, and if we lose sight of the background against which man plays his part we lose much of the essence of the drama. Therefore, the nature of the country must be taken into account. It is a commonplace to say that civilisation can develop only where the soil is such that people can make their livelihood so easily

8

as to enjoy a modicum of leisure; where the climate is not too hot, or too cold, to make work possible all the year round; where there is room for expansion, so that the population can be numerous enough to ensure its protection against attack; where communication is possible with the outside world, so as to facilitate the exchange of goods and of ideas, and where raw materials are accessible for manufacture. How far does southern Mesopotamia answer to these conditions ?

To anyone who to-day visits southern Iraq it must seem strange that this unpromising land should have been the birthplace and the seat of a great civilisation. Not far north of Basra the marshes with their shallow brackish waters and tangled reed-beds fill all the space between the eastern and the western deserts. Above them stretches the vast expanse of flat country through which flows the river Euphrates; a scanty belt of palm-trees fringes its high embankment, tilled fields may extend for a mile or two from the stream or may dwindle to nothing; only where the irrigation canals bring water from the river can anything grow, and here there is no strip of herbage to divide the desert from the sown; the green of the corn-land ends abruptly on a clean-cut line, and beyond it, as far as the eye can see, lies a flat dead world of yellow sand or salt-spangled grey mud whose monotony is relieved only by the low mounds that shroud dead cities. And the people? Housed in low tunnel-like cabins of reed matting or in the yet more squalid mud huts of the villages strung out along the river-bank, the Arabs who wrest their livelihood from the soil, working it with wooden ploughs drawn by camel or ass, guiding the blinkered ox on his endless round above the wheel that raises water for the fields, clearing the ditches of their silted mud with the broad-

bladed hoe and trampling out the grain on the mud thresh-
ing-floor and tossing it with a winnowing-fan against the
wind, they may seem to give no more hope of progress than
does the land itself. And yet, the desert once was green; the
sand-shrouded cities were once populous; here civilisation
flourished, and in the shelter of a rich and ordered life the
arts and crafts were brought to a premature perfection.

But in the beginning the delta was not habitable at all;
the whole of it was one vast shallow inlet of the sea. Then
the silt, which the floods brought down from the Anatolian
hills and deposited in the Gulf where the sea waters slackened
their current, formed a bar enclosing a stagnant lagoon which,
as the silt filled it and the salt water turned to brackish with
the intake from Tigris and Euphrates, became a marsh densely
overgrown with giant reeds. Gradually the edges of the
marsh dried, and islands formed in it, and the dry land, all
water-born silt enriched by the decayed vegetation, was
astonishingly fertile. The dwellers in the north saw what
seemed to them a miracle, saw the creation of a new world,
as 'the waters were gathered together into one place and the
dry land appeared, yielding herbs after their kind'. It was
a desirable land, and they were not slow to take possession
of it.

This miracle of creation took place comparatively late in
human history. The immigrants who moved downstream
into the delta were living in the later phase of the New Stone
Age. They were not nomad huntsmen but agriculturists;
they were primitive, but possessed none the less a culture
of their own so distinctive that wherever their settlements
are found the modern excavator has no doubt of their identity.
It is not yet possible to say to what racial stock they belonged,
but that they were a northern people is certain; a culture

identical with that at al 'Ubaid extends over northern Iraq and across to Syria, and a branch of kindred stock occupied the Persian highland and founded the city of Susa. If, as is likely, they spoke the language which later was that of the historical Sumerians, their northern origin is the more assured, because it is an agglutinative tongue structurally similar to Old Turkish and to Mongolian and Chinese. On sites far to the north, in the neighbourhood of Mosul, the antecedents of the delta settlers can be traced back to their savage beginnings. But those who came to Ur were already in the flower of the al 'Ubaid period. Their most character-istic product, which is indeed the hall-mark of the age, is the finely-painted pottery of which examples are shown on Pl. 1. All the tools used by the al 'Ubaid people were of stone; their settlements are littered with vast numbers of flint hoes used for tilling the soil, flint scrapers for cleaning skins, flint knives for all purposes, drills of flint or obsidian for leather-work. They kept flocks of sheep and goats and spun the wool and wove it into cloth, though the men pre-ferred to wear a kilt of sheepskin cured with the fleece still on it. Men and women alike loved to wear strings of beads, simple discs chipped out of soapstone, shell or yellow car-nelian. They grew barley and harvested it with sickles of burnt clay and ground the grain on flat or saddle-shaped stone querns. They caught fish in the marshes. Those who elected to live on the margin of the higher desert looking over the old marshland built themselves houses of mud brick; the marsh dwellers were perforce content with such reed huts as shelter the marsh Arab of to-day. We may assume that the first incomers were adventurers, single families who pushed down into the new land and settled by themselves on any patch of soil that had risen above the waters and gave promise of an easy livelihood. But as time went on and as the arable land increased in acreage, families grouped themselves together in villages and even in towns. This was inevitable. The fields, fertile as they were, had to be irrigated and drained if that fertility was to endure, and this was more than the isolated peasant farmer could undertake; it required corporate effort, not only numbers, but organised numbers; and so from the needs of agriculture there developed a social system whose natural outcome was an urban economy. Moreover as the network of canals became more complex and the recession of the marsh made water of ever greater value, quarrels would arise as to the ownership of the canals and prior rights to the water that they brought. So wars began between neighbouring communities, and men whose daily work was in the fields found it safer to spend the night in good company behind walls that might safeguard them from attack. The village developed into the walled city.

This took time. At Warka the accumulation of superimposed ruins of the al 'Ubaid period is such that it must represent at least two or three centuries of urban life; at Ur too the town had risen to a considerable height as new houses were built above the levelled remains of the old. But this long growth was to come to a sudden end. At Ur, digging against the northern margin of the al 'Ubaid town, the excavators came upon a bed of clean silt eleven feet thick which had been deposited by a flood whose waters had broken against the obstruction of the town mound. Below the silt were the remains of houses which those waters had destroyed in their first onset. Mesopotamia ia a land of floods, but in all its later history there is no record of such a flood as this; for that heaped silt to form, there must have been twenty or twenty-five feet of water, which would have covered the whole of the delta between the Iraqi desert and the foothills of Elam, and from Hillah, which is Babylon, to the Persian Gulf. This can be none other than the Deluge which was the subject of the most famous of Babylonian legends, the Hebrew version of which is familiar to us all in the story of Noah's Flood.

The Deluge must have destroyed all the villages and scattered farms, all the inhabitants of the open country. It spared the larger towns which, high on their artificial hills, overtopped the waste of waters; but those who survived the disaster were a weakened and a dispirited remnant. Once more the Delta was an empty land, crying out for a population to re-create its fertile fields, to clear its clogged canals and re-plant its palm-groves and gardens. Once more there were people ready to accept the call.

The transition from the period of al 'Ubaid to the period of Uruk is not marked, so far as archaeology can tell, by any signs of violent conquest; the newcomers came in peaceably and were perhaps not unwelcome. Again we do not know exactly who they were, but they too were northerners, a hill people, not savages but possessed of arts and crafts of their own which were speedily grafted on to the indigenous culture of al 'Ubaid. The transition is curiously illustrated at Ur. In a pit dug there, there was found the rubbish-deposit of a potter's factory which began business shortly after the Flood and was active for some generations after that. The earliest refuse in the deepest levels is composed of broken fragments of characteristic late al 'Ubaid pottery—mostly unpainted wares, as if the demand for the old painted vases had fallen off; all was hand-made or turned in a slowly-revolving stand. Then, mixed with these at a higher level, there began to occur examples of the Uruk wares, plain red or smoky grey, spun on the wheel, and amongst the pottery fragments there was found an actual potter's wheel, a thick disc of clay about three feet across with a hole near the rim for the peg handle by which it was spun, and heavy enough to go on revolving of its own momentum. Above this all the pottery was wheel-made. Here was visual proof of a revolutionary change, of the machine superseding the pure handicraft; and that the introduction of the wheel was due to the Uruk people there can be no doubt at all. Nor was this their only contribution. They were metal-workers, and with their arrival the Stone Age in Mesopotamia came to an end, and a natural bronze alloy took the place of flint. They had been builders in stone when they lived in their own hill country of the North, and although stone was hard to come by in the land formed by the Two Rivers they still clung for tradition's sake to its use; the art of stone working was familiar to them. They quickly became masters of the land, but it would seem that they mixed freely with the old al 'Ubaid people and were not ashamed to learn what could profit them from the experience of the older race.

A remarkable proof of the continuity of tradition from the al 'Ubaid period to later times is given by the architecture.

The most primitive building of the marsh settlers was the reed hut, and it was built in this way. Bundles of tall reeds lashed together were planted in the ground in two parallel rows; the tops of each pair of these fascines were bent inwards and tied together so as to form a series of arches, and then other bundles were lashed horizontally to the uprights to make a solid framework. On to the inside of this framework were tied woven reed mats; if wood was used at all it was only for the door and door frame. The effect given was that of panels separated by attached columns. The early builders

14

in mud brick simply translated this into their own material; the only difference was that with square-moulded bricks the attached columns tended to become pilasters, or buttresses, which might be either simple or double; and all through Mesopotamian history no temple or building of the sort was ever set up which did not by its recessed and buttressed walls recall the reed hut of the al 'Ubaid period. Again, the palm-trunk inevitably gave to the earliest settlers the idea of a column to uphold, for example, a porch or door-lintel. The Uruk builders translated this into a brick column covered with an incrustation of coloured clay studs set in patterns which suggested the frond-bases of the palm trunk; in the First Dynasty temple found at Ur (on the al 'Ubaid site) actual palm logs encrusted with stone and bitumen and mother-of-pearl were used (see Pl. 3); and, much later, in about 1950 B.C., a king of Larsa flanked the gateway which he added to the Ziggurat terrace at Ur with free columns of moulded mud brick imitating the palm-tree's surface in every detail.

This continuity of tradition certainly implies that the old inhabitants were not simply reduced to slavery, much less exterminated, by the Uruk invaders; the two stocks assimilated, and if we may judge by the material evidence of their civilisation, best exemplified by the wonderful discoveries made at Warka, it was from their union that the real Sumerian people was born.

Uruk was at the height of its power, its rulers spending their wealth in spacious buildings magnificently adorned, when suddenly a new people appeared upon the Mesopotamian scene. At Ur have been found many graves of these 'Jemdet Nasr' people. They are distinguished by a type of painted pottery of which the chief characteristic is a geometrical pattern painted in buff and black against a deep red background—it has no precedent in any of the older Mesopotamian wares. Another feature of the graves is their extraordinary wealth of stone vases, pots and bowls and cups of limestone, steatite or translucent alabaster-like calcite got from stalagmitic deposits in the Persian Gulf. They were great workers in shell, using the core of the big conch shells which also came from the Persian Gulf. They developed, if they did not actually introduce, the art of writing. The earliest inscribed clay tablets, which are purely pictographic, date back as early as the Uruk period; but even so may be due to the earliest Jemdet Nasr incomers. But in the Jemdet Nasr age pictographs give place to a true linear script in which the signs are identical with those of the cuneiform writing of historic times. It is tempting to connect these Jemdet Nasr immigrants, with their undoubted associations with the Persian Gulf, with the mysterious and only half-human beings who according to late legends entered Sumer coming up from the sea, and introduced to a still semi-barbarous people 'the arts of writing, of agriculture, in fact all the arts'. One thing about them we can safely assert. Whether they came in by armed conquest or, as is more probable, by infiltration, in the end they made themselves masters of the whole south country, for the evidence of their culture occurs throughout the length and breadth of it, though it fails in some of the northern sites; and it is certain too that the tyranny of their rule at last drove the old inhabitants who were their subjects to open rebellion. Not only does the characteristic Jemdet Nasr pottery with its rich decoration in colour disappear abruptly, giving place to plain red and grey wares reminiscent of the Uruk period, but almost always the buildings of the latest Jemdet Nasr phase bear the marks of destruction by fire; usually they have been deliberately razed to the ground and replaced by new constructions. The new buildings erected by the victorious champions of the old order invariably possess one peculiar feature: the bricks of which they are constructed are not of the flat type used in all previous ages and familiar to us to-day, but are round-topped like cakes, an impractical shape for which there is no technical justification. Very often, especially where the new building is a temple, great quantities of broken sherds of al 'Ubaid painted pottery have been collected and mixed with the mud mortar. It is perhaps not too fanciful to see in the adoption of the 'plano-convex' brick a symbol of national revulsion against anything that the hated Jemdet Nasr people had used, and in the al 'Ubaid potsherds, representing the beginnings of Sumer, an affirmation of the tradition whose continuity had been for a time so rudely interrupted. The early Dynastic period, which now begins, though it preserves the art of writing owed to Jemdet Nasr, is in all other branches of culture a direct descendant of the Uruk age.

Such, in outline, is the history that leads up to the Royal Tombs and to the First Dynasty of Ur.

One has to picture now the whole river valley (and indeed the steppe country to the north, bordering the Middle Euphrates) as divided up between a number of small city-states each boasting its capital town and owning a more or less extensive domain of rich farmland watered by a network of laboriously maintained canals.

The racial elements which made up the population were perhaps not equally distributed, but none the less all alike from Mari in the extreme north-west to Eridu in the south had a common culture and a common language, and racial distinctions counted for little. If the states were divided against each other it was by historic tradition and by the rivalries and ambitions of their royal houses. Each city-state had its own kingly ruler. But under the guise of royalty, the basis of the social system was theocratic. The same religion prevailed throughout the whole land, but each state had one of the common pantheon for its particular patron deity, and that deity was the real king, the earthly ruler being content to entitle himself 'the tenant farmer of the god'. When two city-states engaged in war, as they often did, usually on the ground of landmarks displaced or of disputes about water rights, it was the god who led his forces to battle. When one city was so far successful in war that its ruler could claim overlordship over all his neighbours and his house could be ranked by the annalists as one of the 'dynasties' of Sumer, then the god of that city became the principal god of the Sumerian pantheon.

It may be that the alien Jemdet Nasr folk had as conquerors for the first time imposed unity upon the quarrelsome little kingships strung along the valley of the Two Rivers; certainly after their day the political history of the country, for many centuries, resolved itself into a record of the rise and fall of overlords who, starting as vassal rulers of a single city, succeeded in casting off the yoke of the paramount state and making themselves masters 'of the four corners of the earth'. Amongst the cities which thus achieved a temporary suzerainty was Ur; but before the First Dynasty of Ur came into being, the rulers of the town, who were still, though they called themselves 'kings', the vassals of some more powerful master governing perhaps from Erech, had attained such wealth and power as could provide them with the tombs now to be described.

Just outside the wall which enclosed the Temenos of Ur, the Sacred Area within which stood the terraced tower of the Moon God and the main temples of his cult, lay an open space which three thousand years before Christ was the burial-place of the citizens of Ur. Later on, in the days of Sargon of Akkad (about 2560 B.C.), the area was used again for the same purpose and the gravediggers disturbed hundreds of the earlier tombs; later still, after 2000 B.C., houses were built over the ancient cemetery, and the discovery of old graves containing treasure induced men to tunnel deep into the soil in search of plunder. Thus, most of the royal tombs we found had been robbed long ago, and the repeated working of the soil had confused the stratification; but none the less was it clear that the original cemetery was a little earlier in date than the First Dynasty of Ur, a dynasty of kings whose historical existence had first been demonstrated by the excavation of the temple at al 'Ubaid set up by A-anni-pad-da, the second of the royal line (see p. 27).

Of more than a thousand graves of the early period only sixteen were royal tombs: the rest were the graves of private citizens dug as near as might be to the resting-place of the semi-divine ruler, just as to-day in a Moslem cemetery the humble headstones cluster round the domed *turbeh* of a religious sheikh. But whereas the ordinary man was buried in a plain coffin at the bottom of a simple shaft, accompanied by such things as he might be expected to need in another life, vessels for food and drink, weapons and personal ornaments, royalty had a ritual entirely of its own.

A great square pit was dug deep into the soil, approached by a downward-sloping ramp. In the pit was built a tomb, of stone or brick, vaulted or domed: it might be a single chamber or it might be a miniature house with three or four rooms and a connecting passage; the inner face of the walls and the chamber floors were smoothly plastered with white cement. This was the tomb proper. Into it the body was brought and laid upon a bier, surrounded by offerings that testified to the wealth of the ruler in his lifetime and might serve his pleasure hereafter; two or three of his more intimate attendants were killed and their bodies set alongside the bier; then the tomb door was walled up. Next, there came down the ramp into the pit, whose earth sides were masked by reed matting, the whole company of those who were to accompany their royal master to the other world; ministers of the household, musicians, dancing women, male slaves and soldiers of the guard, even the chariot drawn by oxen or by asses, with the drivers, the grooms and the animals, assembled in ordered ranks at the bottom of the pit. Presumably some kind of service was held (in Queen Shub-ad's grave the fingers of the girl harpist were still touching the strings of the lyre), and at its end each took a little cup, filled it might be from a great bronze vessel set in the pit's centre, and drank a draught of a narcotic and lay down in his place and slept. And, from above, the mourners threw in the earth of the pit's making and buried the sleepers and the tomb chamber, and stamped the earth down and made of it a level floor for the next stage of the ceremony. For the filling of the pit was a slow process, done in stages. On the floor, still deep below the ground's surface, there was held a funeral feast and then two or three more human victims were sacrificed and laid out, and more earth was flung in and trodden down, for the same ritual to be repeated two or three times until the shaft was filled up level with the surrounding soil; probably, though for this we have no certain evidence, a funerary chapel was built above-ground to mark the spot, a chapel in which offerings would be made to the memory of the dead and services conducted in his honour.

This generalised description is no flight of fancy: it is based throughout on evidence afforded by the tombs themselves. In the case of PG 1054 we dug down methodically through floor after floor in the filling of the pit, each with its votive deposits and subsidiary burials, till we reached the little domed stone chamber with its blocked door, against which had been put the bones of sacrificed animals, and found inside it the gold-bedecked body with its dead attendants. In Queen Shub-ad's grave the musician with her harp and the singers formed a group apart; the grooms were there with the gaily-adorned and inlaid sledge-chariot drawn by two asses; the Keeper of the Wardrobe lay beside the flat chest which had held the royal dresses. Inside the tomb chamber the ladies-in-waiting were crouched beside the bier on which their mistress lay shrouded in beads of gold and lapis lazuli and carnelian, wearing over her elaborately adorned wig the massive gold hair-ribbon, the gold chaplets and the five-flowered hair-pin of a queen, while on a shelf at her side was put another court wig bound by a broad fillet of lapis lazuli against which were set marvellously-wrought little gold figures of animals and fruit and ears of corn.

The queen's grave had been dug in the shaft of a slightly older tomb, perhaps that of her husband whose last resting-place she wished to share. The grave-diggers had hit upon the vaulted roof of the old king's chamber and, tempted too far, had broken in and plundered it of all its wealth, and had placed the queen's wardrobe chest over the hole to hide the evidence of their misdoing. But they had not disturbed the 'death-pit'. There we found all in order. Eight soldiers with spears and helmets lay in a double rank at the ramp's foot. Facing the ramp (evidently it had been backed down the slope) was the heavy chariot drawn by oxen wearing silver collars, the reins, decorated with huge lapis-lazuli beads, attached to silver rings in their nostrils. The drivers and soldier attendants were with the car. Against the wall of the tomb-chamber were the harpist and the singers; soldiers guarded the walled-up door and stood against the matting-draped sides of the pit; there were 63 persons gathered there to die. In another case, PG 1237, the floor of the death-pit was covered with bodies all in ordered rows: 6 men on the entrance side and 68 women in court dress, red coats with beaded cuffs and shell-ring belts, head-dresses of gold or silver, great lunate ear-rings and multiple necklaces of blue and gold. Amongst them was one girl who was not wearing her silver hair-ribbon,—it was in her pocket, tightly coiled up like a roundel of tape, as if she had been late for the funeral and had not had time to put it on. Here there were four harpists with their lyres, grouped together, and by them in an open space lay a copper cauldron; it was difficult not to connect this with the little drinking-bowl found by every one of the 74 bodies in the pit.

None of the private graves in the cemetery had anything corresponding to this wholesale slaughter. Even the richest of them, the grave of Mes-kalam-dug, which contained a princely wealth of arms and vessels in gold, silver, bronze and stone, had in it no bodies other than that of 'the lord of the good land' himself, solitary in a wooden coffin. The built grave-chamber and the human sacrifice were a privilege reserved for kings. It seems to imply a belief that those kings were at least semi-divine beings for whom death was but a transition; and if we may judge from the fact that so many people died with them without violence, to the accompaniment of music made by themselves and by means of a narcotic voluntarily drunk, surely these people were buoyed up by the confidence that going thus in their lord's company they assured themselves of a continuance of their service and of an honourable place in that other world.

In all the Sumerian literature that we possess there is no hint of any such ritual forming part of the funeral of a king; and since the discovery at Ur was unique of its kind some scholars were loth to accept any such interpretation of the evidence. They pointed out that the few names recovered from the 'Royal Tombs' did not figure in the lists of kings recorded by Sumerian annalists. The facts of the burials were beyond dispute, but they preferred to see in them a sacrifice offered to the acknowledged gods, a 'Fertility rite' in which a mystic marriage symbolising the earth's fruitfulness culminated with the killing of the bride and bridegroom. The first point is true enough. But the Sumerian annalists enumerate only the kings of those dynasties which claimed to rule the whole land of Sumer. The occupants of our Royal Tombs make no such claim, but they do call themselves 'kings'. Their names are not unlike those of the First Dynasty kings—they might well belong to the same family—but judging by the archaeological evidence they are older in date and, if so, were necessarily not dynastic kings but vassals, lords only of a single city. If they were the chosen victims of a 'Fertility rite' they would scarcely call themselves kings at all.

Further, Sumerian literature, which is rich in liturgical and religious texts, gives no hint whatsoever that there was any killing of the protagonists of a 'mystic marriage' rite;

no human sacrifice is suggested anywhere as part of the orthodox religion. The assumption of the 'Fertility rite' therefore does just as much violence to the literary evidence as does the assumption that these are royal burials—more, in fact, for there is no description of any royal burial anywhere in Sumerian literature. Again, the 'mystic marriage' involves two people, bride and bridegroom, and if they had to be killed surely they would be buried together. But each of the Royal Tombs at Ur contains only one principal body. Yet a further argument is this: the need for the fruits of the earth is constant, and if a 'Fertility rite' is practised at all it should be a yearly ceremony, as indeed it was in Sumer in historic times. But in the graveyard at Ur, which must have been in use for many generations, there are only 16 'Royal Tombs'. Did men only 16 times in all those years take steps to secure a good harvest? And now the evidence of the Royal Tombs no longer stands alone. At Ur we have found that a thousand years later the great rulers of the Third Dynasty at Ur had vast tombs just outside the Temenos wall wherein numerous people were buried with them, tombs surmounted by a palace-temple in which the eldest son of the house maintained the worship of the king who was deified in his lifetime and counted as a god after his death. It was an enduring tradition, though literature is silent regarding it, whereby God's 'tenant farmer' partakes of his divinity and does not die but is translated to the heavens.

Here then, in this prehistoric cemetery at Ur, we have the graves of kings and commoners to teach us something of the thoughts and beliefs of a people who have left us no real written testimony of themselves, and to tell us very much about their arts and crafts and the material setting of their lives. Only in one respect does the evidence here compare poorly with that from other sites—we have not found such portrait statues as were unearthed in great numbers at Tell Asmar in northern Iraq in the course of the American excavations there. The reason is that at Ur the site is a cemetery, whereas the building at Tell Asmar was a temple. To the ancient Sumerians, a statue was the last thing one would think of putting in a tomb. A statue represented either a god, in which case the shrine was the obvious place for it, or the human worshipper, and the proper place for the worshipper too was in the temple, where he might stand day and night before his god in perpetual adoration and prayer. For a complete picture of Sumer as it was five thousand years ago we must collect our evidence not from one only but from many sources which in recent years archaeology has opened up to us; but none the less the objects from the cemetery of Ur bear full witness to the quality of the civilisation which had been developed in the Euphrates valley throughout the periods of al 'Ubaid, Uruk and Jemdet Nasr and was flourishing at the dawn of the historic age.

PLATE I

POTTERY OF THE AL 'UBAID PERIOD

The al 'Ubaid 'Flood period' pottery is well illustrated by these examples. The commonest shapes are the flat plate, the flat-footed bowl, and the round-based bowl flattened slightly to an oval and with the rim pushed down and out at one end into a rudimentary spout.

The vessels are hand-made, sometimes completely so, sometimes to a modified degree, the lumps of clay being placed on a pivoted stand which could be turned with one hand while the pot was being shaped with the other—but the stand only moved at the rate of the hand and did not revolve of its own momentum, so that it had none of the essential character of a potter's wheel. The pottery is astonishingly good, and the walls are sometimes of almost egg-shell thinness. The body clay was covered with a light slip or wash of white, and the painted decoration was applied before firing. The decoration is always very simple, but is admirably adapted to the vessel's lines. The kiln was ill regulated; often vessels are found which have been distorted and vitrified in the kiln, and it is common for the white to have assumed a greenish colour owing to over-firing. In spite of that technical weakness it can be said that artistically the earliest pottery of Sumer is the best. Later on the use of stone or metal for luxury vessels killed pottery-making as an art, and the dull mass-produced wares of the potters of the historic ages have no merit other than utility.

PLATE 2

RECONSTRUCTION OF THE TEMPLE AT AL 'UBAID

Al 'Ubaid, a little mound lying four miles north of the city of Ur, gave its name to the pre-Flood pottery of which quantities strewed the ground's surface, evidence of a prehistoric settlement. But the mound itself was made up of the ruins of a little temple of much later date. Amongst the mass of fallen 'plano-convex' bricks (see

p. 17) was found the dedication-stone, a small tablet bearing the inscription, in archaic characters, 'A-anni-pad-da king of Ur, son of Mes-anni-pad-da king of Ur, has built this for his lady Nin-kharsag'.

The name A-anni-pad-da was new to us, but Mes-anni-pad-da was familiar as the first king of what the Sumerian annalists called the First Dynasty of Ur; the tablet proved for the first time the historical existence of this dynasty, which must have borne sway somewhere about 3000 B.C.

The temple stood on a platform built of sun-dried bricks with a buttressed facing of burnt brick resting on rough limestone foundations (see p. 14); it was approached by a flight of finely-cut limestone stairs, the outside of the staircase being panelled with wood. The platform was preserved virtually to its full height, but of its super-structure, the temple proper, nothing was left *in situ*; it had been violently overthrown and its mud-brick walls razed to their foundations. But against the platform's foot great masses of those walls lay one above another, and to their underside there still adhered the elements of the decoration of the temple façade; by planning each wall fragment, its position and the angle at which it lay, and each piece of ornament exactly as it had fallen, it was possible to fix the place of each in relation to the others, and so to work out a fairly accurate reconstruction of the original façade.

The stone steps led to a level stair-head covered by an open porch which was upheld by columns made of palm-logs sheathed in copper and roofed with slenderer copper-plated timbers. The porch projected from a shallow pylon or gate-tower, a feature which was to be traditional in Sumerian ecclesiastical architecture. The doorway was flat-topped and its jambs probably were splayed with double reveals, and against them stood on either side of the entrance a column of palm-wood overlaid with mosaic (see Pl. 3) supporting as architrave a great copper relief which bore the heraldic design of an eagle grasping with its claws two antlered stags; the relief was hammered out of sheet metal but the heads were hollow castings in the round, made separately and riveted to the background. The doorway itself was flanked by life-size figures of lions made of copper beaten over a wooden core, with inlaid eyes and teeth and tongues.

27

The gate-tower stood flush with the platform's edge: the wall of the shrine proper therefore was set back a little, and along this ledge there stood a row of statues of oxen made of copper beaten over wooden cores; they stood in profile, but their heads were turned outwards to the spectator. Behind them the lower part of the temple façade was decorated with rosettes, clay pegs with flowers of alternate white and red petals attached with bitumen and copper wire. In the drawing these are shown standing upright and free, which was what the evidence seemed to me to indicate; but parallels found later on other sites prove that my view was wrong, and the flower-stems were embedded in the brickwork with only the heads showing, flush with the wall surface. Above this ran a frieze of copper bulls, the animals represented as reclining but in the act to rise, in profile, with the head turned outwards. Here again the bodies are repoussés in relief, and the heads, cast in the round, are attached. Higher up the wall was a second frieze. This had a copper frame within which were figures cut out in white shell or in limestone and silhouetted against a mosaic background of black shale. There is a very striking difference between the shell figures, which are beautifully made, modelled in delicate relief and finely polished, and the limestone figures, which are rougher and lacking in detail in spite of the fact that they belong to the most important part of the frieze ; it seems probable that whereas the shell was left white, the limestone was painted. The subject of the frieze is a scene on the temple farm: a long procession of cattle advances to the centre, where they are being milked in front of the byre—a typical construction of logs and reed matting. Shaven temple servants squat on the ground under the cows' tails and milk them from behind: others carry off the milk and pass it through a strainer and pour it into a great stone jar.

The procession of cattle is interrupted only by a curious square panel showing a bearded bull attacked by a lion-headed eagle; this is a mythological subject which would be out of place if the rest were only what it seems, a simple pastoral scene, itself scarcely suited for the adornment of a temple. There can be little doubt but that the whole is symbolic, and on the temple farm the priests of Nin-kharsag are preparing the milk of the Mother Goddess which was the life-giving nectar of kings.

Higher up on the wall was another frieze, limestone doves (these were roughly silhouetted and must certainly have been painted) against the usual black shale background. The whole building was gay and fanciful, with the gleaming copper of its statues and reliefs, its many-coloured mosaic columns, its rosettes and its painted friezes in bands against the whitewashed wall face; very sophisticated, the scheme of its decoration obeying a recognised rule of perspective whereby at the base, virtually at eye-level, came the figures in the round, then the reliefs, then the modelled mosaic frieze and above them all the flat silhouetted birds. It was no primitive art that produced the rococo temple of Nin-Kharsag, but an art fully developed, experimented and almost decadent.

PLATE 3

SECTION OF COLUMN FROM THE DOORWAY
OF THE AL 'UBAID TEMPLE

The incrustation is in mother-of-pearl, red limestone and black bituminous shale. Each triangle has at the back two convergent holes forming a loop through which was put a piece of copper wire whose ends were then twisted together: this was to act as a hold-fast securing the incrustation to its background, a thick bed of bitumen ...d over the palm-log of the column proper.

... olumn lay on its side, and with the complete disappearance ...d and the reduction of the bitumen to dry powder, had bee... ...uite flat, but the tesserae lay in their order. Waxed or glued cloth was fixed to them and each side of the column could be lifted in a single sheet and applied to a new core without any disturbance of the tesserae in their relation to each other. The present core is a petrol tin, which was found to be of exactly the right dimensions.

THE STANDARD OF UR

This remarkable object was found lying against the shoulder of an attendant in a royal tomb-chamber. It was made of wood, like a box with sloping rectangular sides measuring 19 × 8 inches, ends in the form of truncated triangles, and a flat base and top. Sides and ends were covered with a mosaic of shell, lapis lazuli and red sandstone set in bitumen; the base and top were plain. It might have been fixed to a pole or staff and have been the top of a ceremonial standard.

When it was found, the wood had all perished and the bitumen had gone to a dry powder. Stones falling from the chamber roof had broken away one corner and had pressed the whole surface of the mosaic out of the flat; but by working carefully, a square inch at a time, it was possible to bind the loose tesserae with hot wax and muslin, to lift each side in one piece and eventually to flatten each panel and fix it to a new background without disturbing or re-setting the minute fragments of which the design is composed; only the broken corner of one panel and the triangular ends (not illustrated here) were seriously dislocated and had to be pieced together afresh.

The two sides of the standard represent respectively War and the Celebration of Victory. On the former, in the top register, is seen the King, distinguished by his stature: he has dismounted from his ass-drawn chariot and soldiers are leading up to him the naked prisoners whom they have just captured. His attendants have battle-axes and light spears. In the second register we have the heavy infantry, drawn up in a phalanx; they wear helmets and kilts over which are heavy capes (probably of felt, like the capes of Anatolian shepherds of to-day) and they are armed with short heavy spears.

In front of them the light infantry, skirmishers, are engaged with the enemy: the Sumerians wear the kilt and helmet—one has a light cloak over his arm,—and carry spears; the enemy are naked, some of them clean-shaven in Sumerian fashion, some wild bearded men coming perhaps from the hills of Elam.

In the lowest register is the chariotry. The body of the chariot made of leather (?) stretched on a wooden frame, is rather like that of a milk-float, high in front, open behind and with a step at the back; the wheels are solid, made of two pieces of wood fixed together with battens or thongs; presumably they had leather tyres, as did the wheels of the chariot we found in the king's grave below that of Queen Shub-ad. The pole is long and high, going above the backs

30

of the four asses which draw the car; at its highest point is fixed the double ring through which the reins pass. Two men are carried in each car, the driver unarmed, and a fighting man armed with a throwing-spear or battle-axe; attached to the front of the car is a quiver containing four spare javelins for the warrior's use. The chariots advance over a field strewn with the enemy dead, and with a touch of realism, the artist shows the effect upon the asses: in the rear they move quietly enough, then as the smell of blood excites them, quicken their pace until the front team is almost out of control and plunges furiously over the corpses.

Not the least interesting feature of this mosaic picture is that it illustrates the armament and the organisation of the earliest field army of which we have any knowledge, the Sumerian army which was destined not only to win mastery of the Euphrates valley towns but to extend its conquests to the Anatolian highlands and to the shores of the Mediterranean. As a historical document it is of prime importance.

On the obverse side of the Standard the Sumerians celebrate their victory. In the top register the King and his son (the main figure has perished) are seated on chairs with the captains of the host facing them, also seated; all wear sheepskin kilts and hold drinking-cups; attendants minister to them, and a player on a lyre and a woman singer supply music. In the other two registers servants bring food for the feast, cattle and goats and fish, and soldiers bring the spoils taken from the enemy, corded bundles, captured teams of asses, and a bound prisoner who may be the general of the beaten army.

PLATE 6

LYRE FROM THE LARGEST ROYAL DEATH-PIT

This is the most magnificent of the four lyres found in the largest royal death-pit. The instrument has now a height of just under 47 inches: the feet, which would have raised it another two inches or more, are lacking. The wood of which it was made had disappeared completely, but it lay flat on its side on the pit's floor with all its component parts in perfect order, so that measurements could be taken with absolute precision and it was possible, by means of wax and cloth, to lift the whole of it in one virtually intact piece. All that was then necessary was to build a new wooden body and attach to it the strips of waxed mosaic. As the illustration shows, the decoration consists of gold and silver, white shell, red limestone and lapis lazuli.

From the front of the sounding-box projects the golden head of a bull wearing an elaborately-curled false beard which is attached by a fastening coming over the muzzle—this may be the attribute of divinity which turns the animal into something more than the beast of the field and makes of it 'The Bull of Heaven'. The sounding-box itself is in the form of the bull's body, highly schematised. Down the front of it was a row of shell plaques engraved with mythological scenes; round the edge of the sides runs a mosaic border. At the base, on one side, the border pattern is interrupted by a slit above which are vertical strips of white and red; probably through this slit were made fast the strings (eight, corresponding to the eight white strips) which, passing over a wooden bridge standing out from the side of the sounding-box, went up to the cross-bar. As the analogy of one of the silver lyres shows, they would be attached to this by loops through which were passed rods the twisting of which tightened and tuned the strings.

This lyre is of the type of that shown in the hands of the musician in the 'banquet scene' of the Royal Standard (Pl. 5).

PLATE 7

THE HELMET OF MES-KALAM-DUG

The grave of Mes-kalam-dug was the richest non-royal grave found in the cemetery. The body lay in a plain wooden coffin, but with the body, and piled against the side and ends of the coffin in the bottom of the grave-shaft, there was an astonishing wealth of weapons, vases, etc., in gold and silver, bronze, stone, and clay. A number of these were inscribed with the name of the dead warrior: the name was the same as that of one of the kings, so he may well have been a scion of the royal house, but he was buried as a commoner without any of the ritual that distinguished a reigning monarch.

Alongside the crushed skull rested this helmet. It is beaten up from a single sheet of 15-carat gold, and is in the form of a wig with the locks of hair hammered out in relief and the hairs chased. Inside it was fitted a quilted cap, fragments of which were found; the cloth had been brought up over the rim of the helmet, so as to protect the wearer's skin from the sharp edges of the metal, and secured by laces passed through the small holes.

PLATE 8

GOLD DAGGER AND RETICULE, FROM A MUCH-RUINED 'DEATH-PIT'

The dagger has a total length of 14½ inches. The hilt is made of a single piece of lapis lazuli decorated with gold studs, and is pierced with a lanyard-hole lined with gold. The blade is of gold and bears a roughly-incised sign which is probably an owner's mark. The sheath is of gold: the back plain, except for two lines of beading, the front of open-work in a design derived from the plaited and woven grass sheaths used for the knives of the common folk.

The little gold reticule is cast in one piece, with horizontal bands of ornament in relief, the motive again being derived from woven-work in grass or fibre. In it was a toilet set consisting of an ear-scoop, a stiletto and tweezers, hung on a ring, all of gold.

PLATE 9

'THE RAM CAUGHT IN A THICKET'

This is one of a pair of figures found lying close to one another in the largest of the royal 'death-pits'. The subject is a goat, 19½ inches high, standing erect with its forefeet against the stem of a flowering shrub to the branches of which it was secured by silver chains (now completely decayed) made fast round its fetlocks. The name 'the ram caught in a thicket' is purely fanciful, but it has this justification, that the theme is not merely decorative but has assuredly some religious content. If, as is not unlikely, the two figures were parts of a single composition and were set facing one another, we should have here an unusually elaborate version of a composition very common in Sumerian art, two animals rampant like heraldic 'supporters'. This is the more likely in that our goats are not pieces of free sculpture; from behind the shoulder of each there rises a solid gold stump which is evidently the base of something that has now disappeared; they are literally 'supporters', though we cannot say of what.

As an example of Sumerian polychrome statuary, the goats are unequalled in our discoveries, and technically they are of great interest. The figure was constructed on a wooden core, of which the head and legs were finely cut, the body more roughly modelled. The face and legs of the animal were covered with thin gold foil hammered against the wood and stuck to it with a thin wash of bitumen; over the body bitumen was laid much more thickly, as a bedding for the heavy incrustation which formed the fleece. Most of this is of shell, each lock of hair being a separate tongue-shaped piece of white shell conventionally engraved; on the neck and shoulders, however, instead of shell, there were curling locks cut in blue lapis lazuli. The beard and horns were of lapis lazuli, the eyes of shell with lapis pupils, the belly of the beast was of silver plate. The small square stand was encrusted with pink and yellow sandstone and white shell.

Fortunately, although the wooden core had decayed away altogether, the work of 'restoration' could be reduced to a minimum. The goat here illustrated lay on its side and had been crushed quite flat but was not broken. By waxing the shell and lapis lazuli and applying muslin, the two sides of the body could be lifted and separated and pressed out again into shape and applied to a new body without the individual tesserae being disturbed; wire and plastic wood could be pushed up the legs and the gold mask could be re-annealed and pressed from the inside into its original form; only the silver of the belly was oxidised beyond recall. The same is true of the tree, of which the gold has been re-set on a wooden stem and branches of copper wire. As a result, the work, and the gold work in particular, lacks the fine finish which more radical measures of restoration might have produced, but there has been virtually no tampering with the maker's handiwork.

PLATE 10

ORNAMENTS FROM A WOMAN'S HEAD-DRESS

This set of ornaments is an unusually fine example of the fashion of the period. The hair was kept in place by a very long broad ribbon of flexible gold. Over this, in front, across the forehead, were fixed these diadems, one above another, the gold pendants of each overlapping the strings of that below it.

The beech-leaves were invariably worn and very often were the only pendants used. The long sallow-like leaves are unusual; the rings and the rather clumsy gold and lapis lazuli disks only occasionally occur. The head-dress was completed by very large lunate ear-rings of gold.

PLATE 11

INLAID GAMING-BOARDS

Four of these boards were found in the graves. All were apparently of the same type, though the decoration of the squares is very different in different examples.

The upper board shown here was very simple, little disks of shell with red or blue centres being set in the bitumen which covered the wood and formed the background. The lower example is much more elaborate, entirely covered with an incrustation of shell plaques inlaid with lapis lazuli and red limestone and divided by lapis lazuli strips; in other examples the majority of the plaques, and also the white 'pieces', are engraved with animal scenes; but all agree in having the coloured rosette in the middle row of the larger section next to the 'bridge'.

The boards were hollow, boxes, in fact, in which were kept the counters or 'pieces', seven black and seven white, and the curious dice, triangular in shape with two of the four points dotted with inlay; three white and three lapis dice made a set, perhaps three for each player. How the game was played we do not know, but clearly the number five was very important, and one may guess that there were lucky and unlucky squares.

PLATE 12

GOLD GOBLET AND BOWL

The gold goblet, $3\frac{1}{2}$ inches high, found in Queen Shub-ad's grave, is strangely Greek in form.

The oval gold bowl, from the grave of Mes-kalam-dug, is $6\frac{1}{3}$ inches long and has lapis lazuli lugs, vertically pierced, between projecting plates of gold: these were for the handle, probably of silver wire. The bowl forms a curious contrast to that in Pl. 13: it has the same fluting and the same rosette chased on the base, but the workmanship is strangely rough and strong.

PLATE 13

GOLD VESSELS FROM QUEEN SHUB-AD'S GRAVE

These vessels are remarkable for their delicate workmanship and fine finish. The tumbler, $6\frac{1}{3}$ inches high, with fluted sides, chased chevron pattern round the rim and base and a rosette on the base, is of a type very common in this period; numerous examples were found in gold, silver and copper. The oval bowl, 5 inches long, with tubular handle-lug, is another superb example of goldsmith's work.

PLATE 14

CUP, WHETSTONE AND BOWL

The little spouted cup, $2\frac{3}{4}$ inches high, and the gold-hung whetstone, are of lapis lazuli; both come from Queen Shub-ad's tomb.

The oval bowl, $8\frac{1}{2}$ inches long and just over 5 inches wide, is of translucent green-veined calcite. Its shape is borrowed from the metal types illustrated in Pls. 12 and 13. It was found in fragments and has been repaired.

Lapis lazuli is not found in Mesopotamia. The stone was imported viâ Persia from the Pamir mountains, and was worked by the craftsmen of Ur. The great quantities of it found in the royal cemetery prove the importance at that early date of an overland commerce carried on over so vast an area and across so many countries. In the cemetery period the natural stone is almost invariably employed; in later and less prosperous times the waste material resulting from the cutting of the stone was re-used, powdered and mixed with some binding fluid to form a paste which when dry gave a good colour but a matt surface. In the Sargonid age this 'reconditioned' lapis lazuli is very common.

PLATE 15

JAR FROM QUEEN SHUB-AD'S TOMB

The jar is 9 inches high; it is cut from a block of translucent veined calcite got from stalagmitic deposits in the Red Sea area.

PLATE 16

REIN-RING FROM THE SLEDGE-CHARIOT OF QUEEN SHUB-AD

The double ring is of silver, the donkey 'mascot' is of electrum, an alloy of silver and gold: it is a solid casting. When found, the figure had been bent over sideways, and the lower forelegs are still somewhat distorted. The inlay of the eyes has perished.

The object was fitted on to the pole of the chariot, to which it was lashed with thongs passed over the four hooks at the base: the reins went through the two loops. Rein-rings of this sort, but without the mascot, are figured on the Royal Standard (Pl. 4). The Queen's chariot was drawn by asses. Her husband's chariot, found lower down (see p. 20), was drawn by oxen, and the rein-ring mascot was a silver ox.

SHORT BIBLIOGRAPHY

Abhandlungen der Preussischen Akademie der Wissenschaften (Berlin). Phil. hist. Klasse, 1929, No. 7. 'Ausgrabungen in Uruk', by Julius Jordan; ditto, 1930, No. 4; ditto, 1932, No. 2; ditto, 1932, No. 6, by E. Heindrich and by A. von Haller.

Abraham. By Sir Leonard Woolley. London, 1936.

Al 'Ubaid. By H. R. Hall and C. Leonard Woolley. London, 1927. (Publications of the Joint Expedition of the British Museum and the Museum of the University of Pennsylvania to Mesopotamia.)

Antiquaries' Journal. V, p. 347, London, 1925; VII, p. 385, 1927; VIII, p. 1, 1928; IX, p. 305, 1929; X, p. 315, 1930; XI, p. 342, 1931; XII, p. 355, 1932; XIII, p. 371, 1933; XIV, p. 4. (Society of the Antiquaries of London.)

Archaeology and the Sumerian Problem. By Henri Frankfort. Chicago, 1932. (University of Chicago. Studies in Ancient Oriental Civilisation, No. 4.)

Délégation en Perse: Mémoires. XIII, 'Ceramique peinte de Suse', by J. de Morgan and R. de Mecquenem. Paris, 1912.

Development of Sumerian Art. The. By Sir Leonard Woolley. London, 1935.

Gazette des Beaux Arts: VIme Période. VIII, Oct. 1932. 'L'Art sumérien archaïque', by L. Legrain.

History and Monuments of Ur. By C. J. Gadd. London, 1929.

Iraq. Vol. III, p. 1; Vol IV, p. 91. By M. E. L. Mallowan. (Journal of the British School of Archaeology in Irak.)

Journal of the Royal Asiatic Society. 'Assyriological Notes,' by Sidney Smith. 1928, p. 849.

Kish. By S. Langdon. Vol. I. Paris, 1924.

Museum Journal (Museum of the University of Pennsylvania). 1924–1933 *passim.*

Music and Letters. X, No. 2. April 1929. 'The Sumerian Harp of Ur,' by Canon F. W. Galpin.

Report on Excavations at Jemdet Nasr: Iraq. By E. Mackay. Field Museum of Natural History, Anthropology, Memoirs. Vol. I, No. 3. Chicago, 1931.

Revue d'Assyriologie et d'Archéologie orientale. XXX, 4. 1933. 'Les Fouilles de Tello', by André Parrot. Paris, 1933.

Royal Anthropological Institute: Occasional Papers: Nos. 6 and 8. 'Studies in Early Pottery in the Near East', by Henri Frankfort.

Sumerian Palace: A. Part II. By Ernest Mackay. Chicago, 1929.

Sumerians: The. By C. Leonard Woolley. Oxford, 1928.

Tell Asmar and Khafaje. By Henri Frankfort, Thorkild Jacobsen and Conrad Preusser. Chicago, 1932.

Ur Excavations. Vol. II, 'The Royal Cemetery', by C. Leonard Woolley. Oxford, 1934. Vol. III, 'Archaic Seal-impressions', by Léon Legrand. Vol. V. 'The Ziggurat and its Surroundings', by Sir Leonard Woolley. Oxford. (Publications of the Joint Expedition of the British Museum and of the Museum of the University of Pennsylvania to Mesopotamia.)

Ur of the Chaldees. By C. Leonard Woolley. London, 1929.

Zeitschrift für Assyriologie. N.F.V. (XXXIX). 'Das Menschenopfer bei den alten Sumerern', by Franz Bohl. Berlin and Leipzig, 1929.

Painted Pottery from Al'Ubaid

The First Dynasty temple at Al'Ubaid; reconstruction of the façade

The temple at Al 'Ubaid. Part of the second frieze; two shell figures set in a background of black shale

4

"The Standard of Ur." War

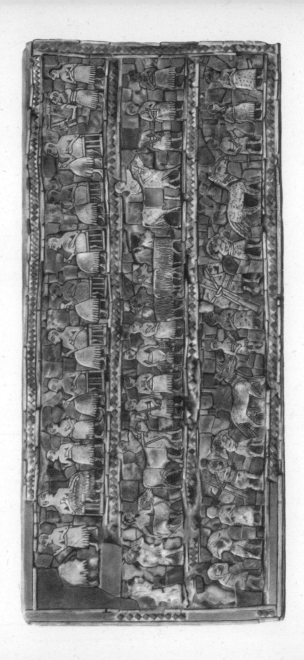

" The Standard of Ur." The victory banquet

The Royal Lyre

The Gold Helmet of Meskalam-dug

The gold dagger of Ur and a gold toilet case

"The Ram caught in a Thicket"

Gold wreaths from Queen Shub-ad's head-dress

Inlaid gaming-boards with the " men " and dice

Gold vessels

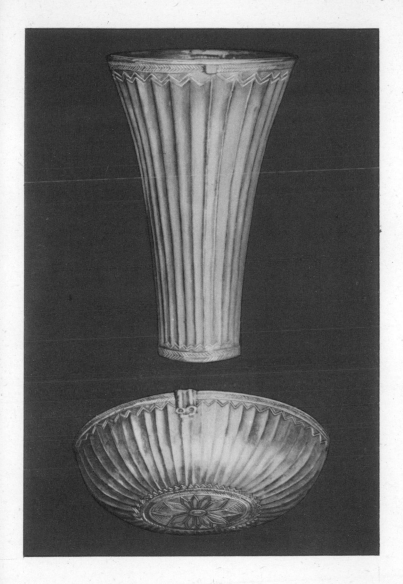

Gold vessels from Queen Shub-ad's tomb

*Bowls of lapis lazuli and green calcite, and
a lapis lazuli whetstone*

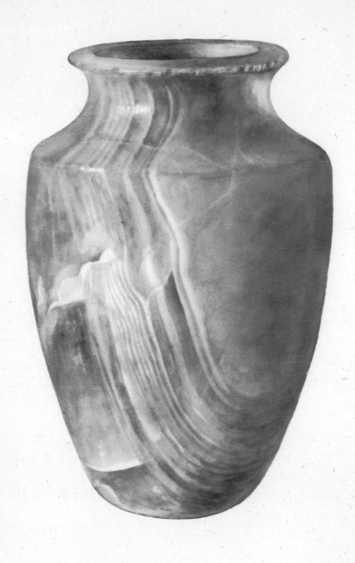

Stone vase from Queen Shub-ad's tomb

Rein-ring and mascot from
Queen Shub-ad's chariot